12

W9-AAZ-644

CUDDLY RABBITS/ CONEJOS ENCANTADORES

By Katie Kawa

Traducción al español: Eduardo Alamán

Gareth Stevens
Publishing

Please visit our website, www.garethstevens.com. For a free color catalog of all our high-quality books, call toll free 1-800-542-2595 or fax 1-877-542-2596.

Library of Congress Cataloging-in-Publication Data

Kawa, Katie.
  [Cuddly rabbits. Spanish & English]
  Cuddly rabbits = Conejos encantadores / Katie Kawa.
     p. cm. — (Pet corner = Rincón de las mascotas)
  Includes index.
  ISBN 978-1-4339-5619-5 (library binding)
  1. Rabbits—Juvenile literature. I. Title. II. Title: Conejos encantadores.
  SF453.2.K3918 2012
  636.932'2—dc22
                                    2011009792

First Edition

Published in 2012 by
Gareth Stevens Publishing
111 East 14th Street, Suite 349
New York, NY 10003

Editor: Katie Kawa
Designer: Andrea Davison-Bartolotta
Spanish Translation: Eduardo Alamán

Photo credits: Cover, pp. 1, 7, 11, 13, 15, 19, 23, 24 (fruit) Shutterstock.com; p. 5 Dorling Kindersley/Getty Images; pp. 9, 24 (digging box) Steve Shott/Dorling Kindersley/Getty Images; p. 17 iStockphoto/Thinkstock; p. 21 David De Lossey/Photodisc/Thinkstock.

Printed in the United States of America

CPSIA compliance information: Batch #CS11GS: For further information contact Gareth Stevens, New York, New York at 1-800-542-2595.

Contents

- -

Contenido

Rabbits live in big cages. They need room to hop!

Los conejos viven en jaulas grandes. ¡Los conejos necesitan espacio para brincar!

Some rabbits have ears that stand up. Some rabbits have ears that go down.

Algunos conejos tienen las orejas paradas. Otros, tienen las orejas caídas.

A rabbit digs in its cage. It uses a digging box.

Este conejo excava en su jaula. Usa una caja para excavar.

Rabbits eat hay
and vegetables.

Los conejos comen
heno y verduras.

Rabbits eat treats too.
One kind of treat
is fruit.

Los conejos también
comen fruta. Este
conejo come una
manzana.

A rabbit plays outside its cage. It runs and jumps.

Este conejo juega fuera de su jaula. El conejo corre y brinca.

Rabbits play every day.
This keeps them healthy.

Los conejos juegan
todos los días. Esto
los mantiene sanos.

Some rabbits are shy.
They hide from people.

Algunos conejos son
tímidos. Estos conejos
se esconden de las
personas.

People talk to rabbits.
This helps them to
stop hiding.

Las personas hablan a
los conejos. Esto hace
que no se escondan.

People have to be careful when they hold a rabbit.

Las personas deben tener mucho cuidado cuando toman a un conejo.

23

Words to Know / Palabras que debes saber

digging box/
(la) caja para excavar

fruit/
(la) fruta

Index / Índice

24